Backyard
Bugs
& Creepy-
Crawlies

Praying Mantids

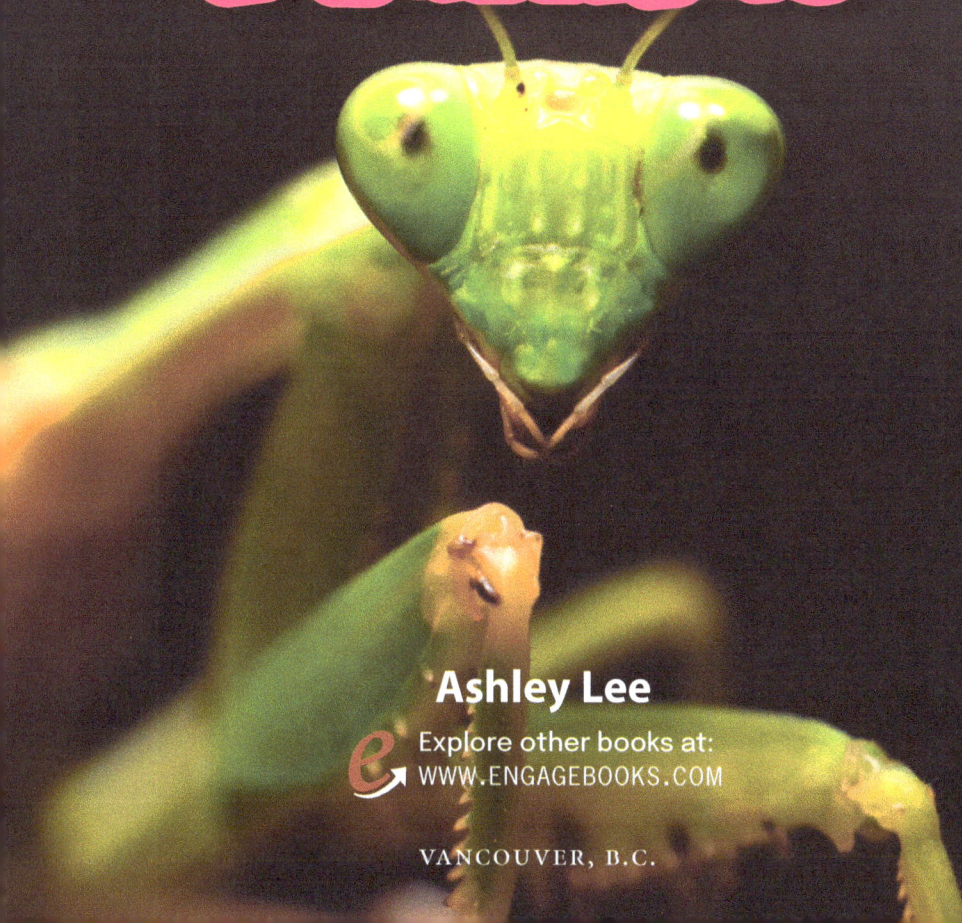

Ashley Lee

Explore other books at:
WWW.ENGAGEBOOKS.COM

VANCOUVER, B.C.

WWW.ENGAGEBOOKS.COM

Praying Mantids: Level 1
Backyard Bugs & Creepy Crawlies
Lee, Ashley 1995 –
Text © 2022 Engage Books
Design © 2022 Engage Books

Edited by: A.R. Roumanis

Text set in Epilogue

FIRST EDITION / FIRST PRINTING

LIBRARY AND ARCHIVES CANADA CATALOGUING IN PUBLICATION

Title: Praying Mantids / Ashley Lee.
Names: Lee, Ashley, author.
Description: Series statement: Backyard bugs & creepy-crawlies
Engaging readers: level 1, beginner.

Identifiers: Canadiana (print) 20250448542 | Canadiana (ebook) 20250448569
ISBN 978-1-77878-707-2 (hardcover)
ISBN 978-1-77878-716-4 (softcover)

Subjects:
LCSH: Praying Mantids—Juvenile literature.

Classification: LCC QL737.P94 C38 2025 | DDC J599.885—DC23

This project has been made possible in part by the Government of Canada.

Canada

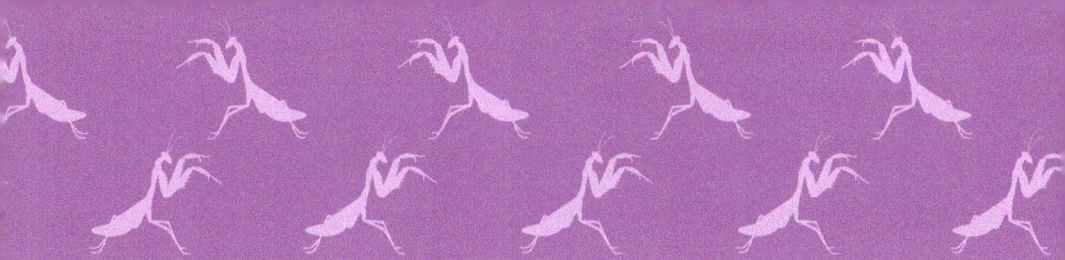

Contents

What Are Praying Mantids?

Praying mantids are insects. There are more than 2,000 kinds of mantids.

4

Some people call praying mantids "praying mantises." Praying mantises are only one kind of praying mantid.

What Do Mantids Look Like?

Many mantids are green or brown. Some are fun colors like pink or purple.

Mantid heads are shaped like triangles. Their eyes stick out on the side.

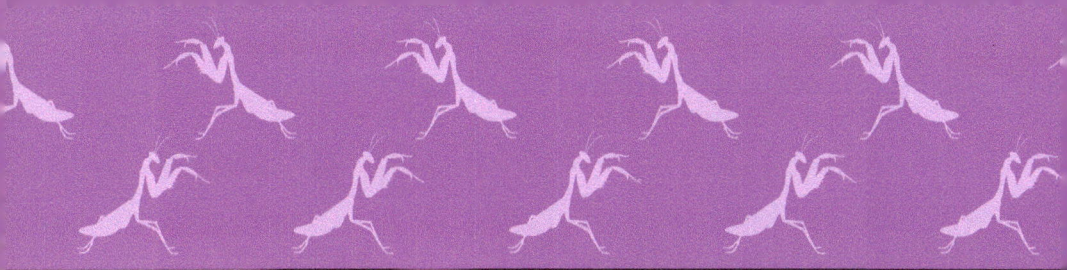

Most mantids have wings. Not all mantids can use their wings.

Mantids only have one ear. It is found between their legs.

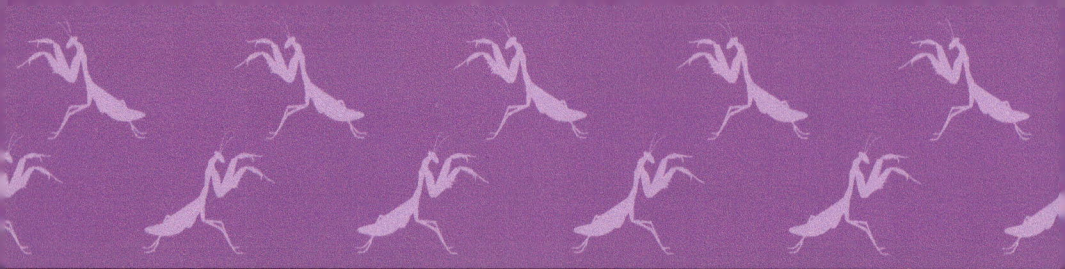

Where Do Mantids Live?

Mantids live in places that have warm weather. They mostly live in **tropical** areas.

Key Word

Tropical: areas that are hot with lots of rain year-round.

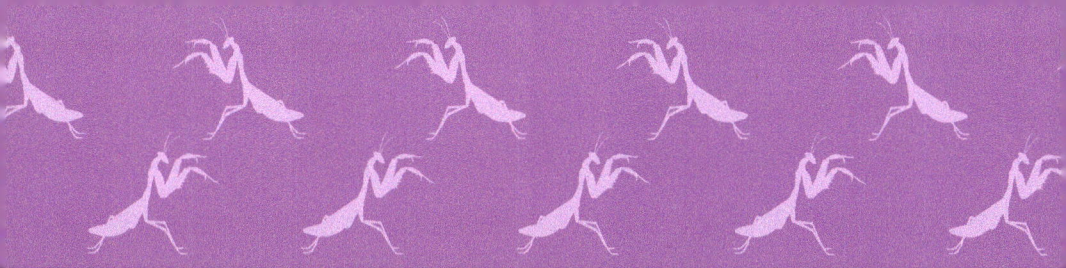

Mantids spend most of their lives on plants like trees or tall grass. Only a few kinds live on the ground.

11

What Do Mantids Eat?

Mantids mostly eat other bugs. They will eat almost anything they can catch.

Some mantids eat small animals like frogs or lizards. Only big mantids do this.

12

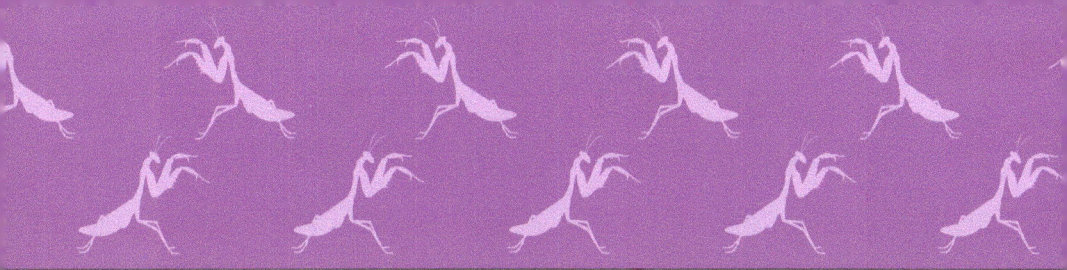

13

Most mantids do not chase their food. They hide and wait until their **prey** gets close.

Key Word

Prey: an animal that is hunted and eaten by another animal.

14

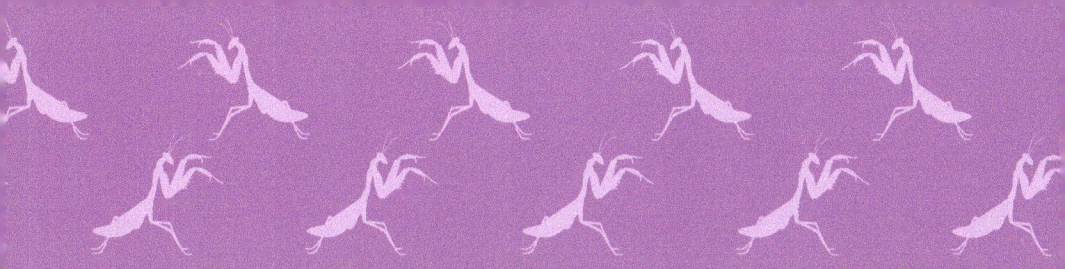

Then they surprise their prey. They grab them with the spikes on their arms.

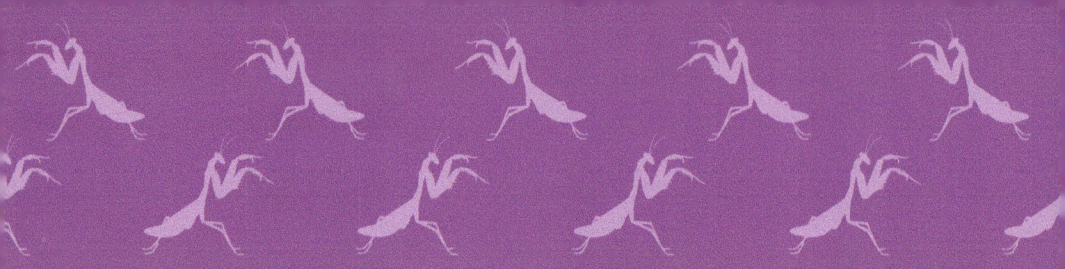

Mantid Behavior

Mantids are good at hiding from other animals. They look just like leaves or sticks.

They often live alone. They will chase other mantids away from their **territory**.

Key Word

Territory: an area that an animal lives in and protects from other animals.

Young mantids shed their skin many times. They get bigger each time they shed their skin.

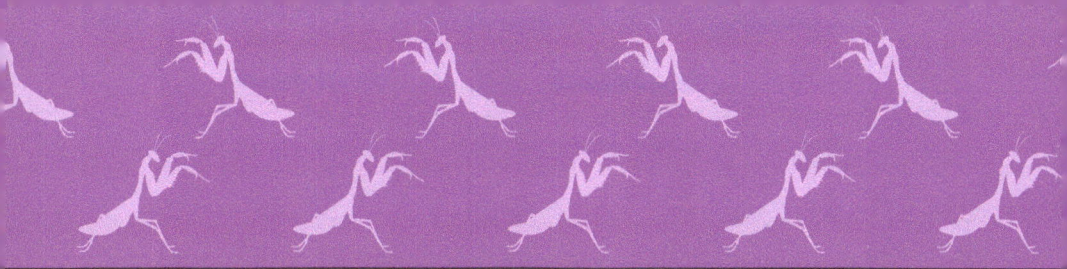

Female mantids sometimes eat male mantids. They only do this if they are really hungry.

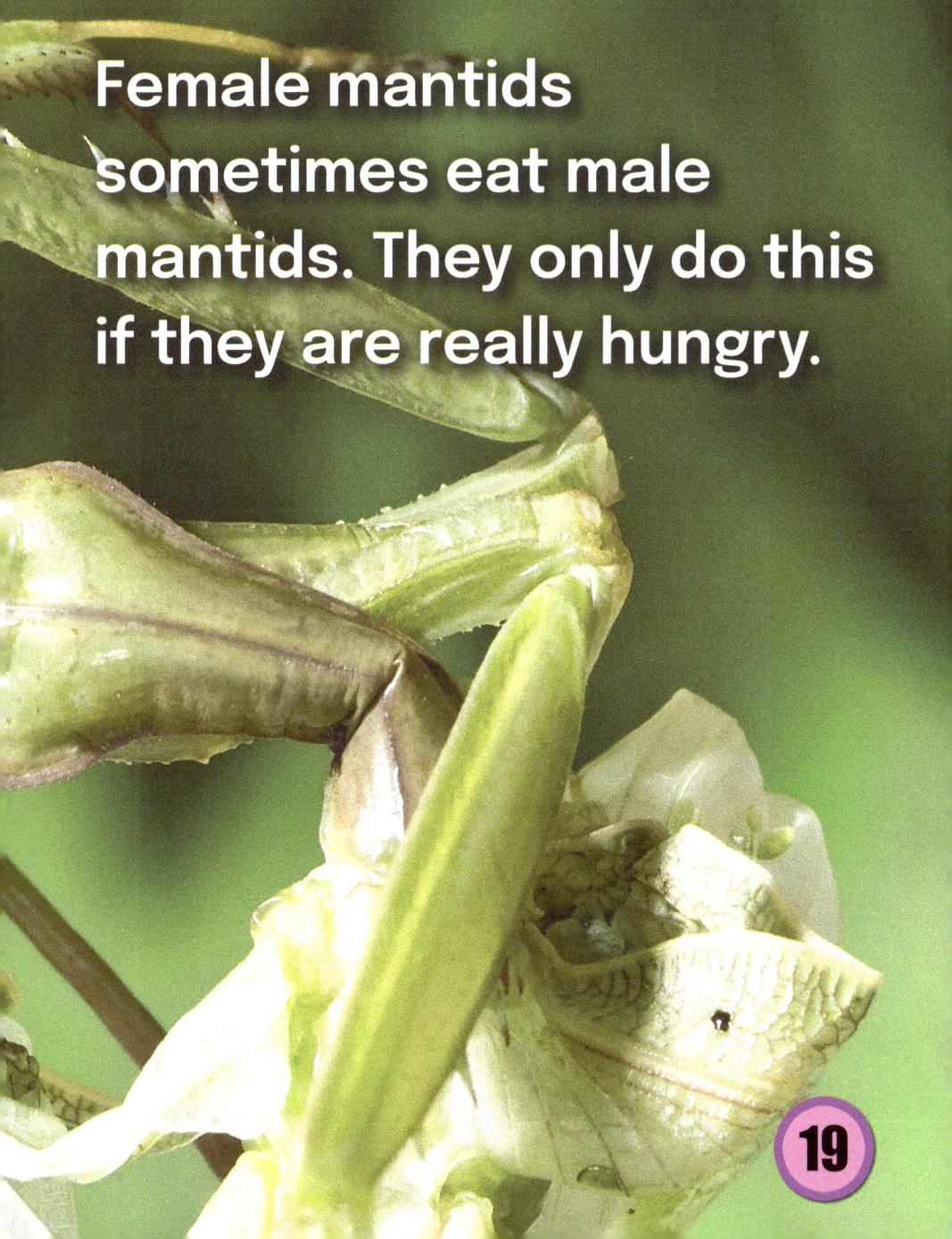

Mantid Life Cycle

Mantids lay eggs in a case called an ootheca. The ootheca keeps them safe.

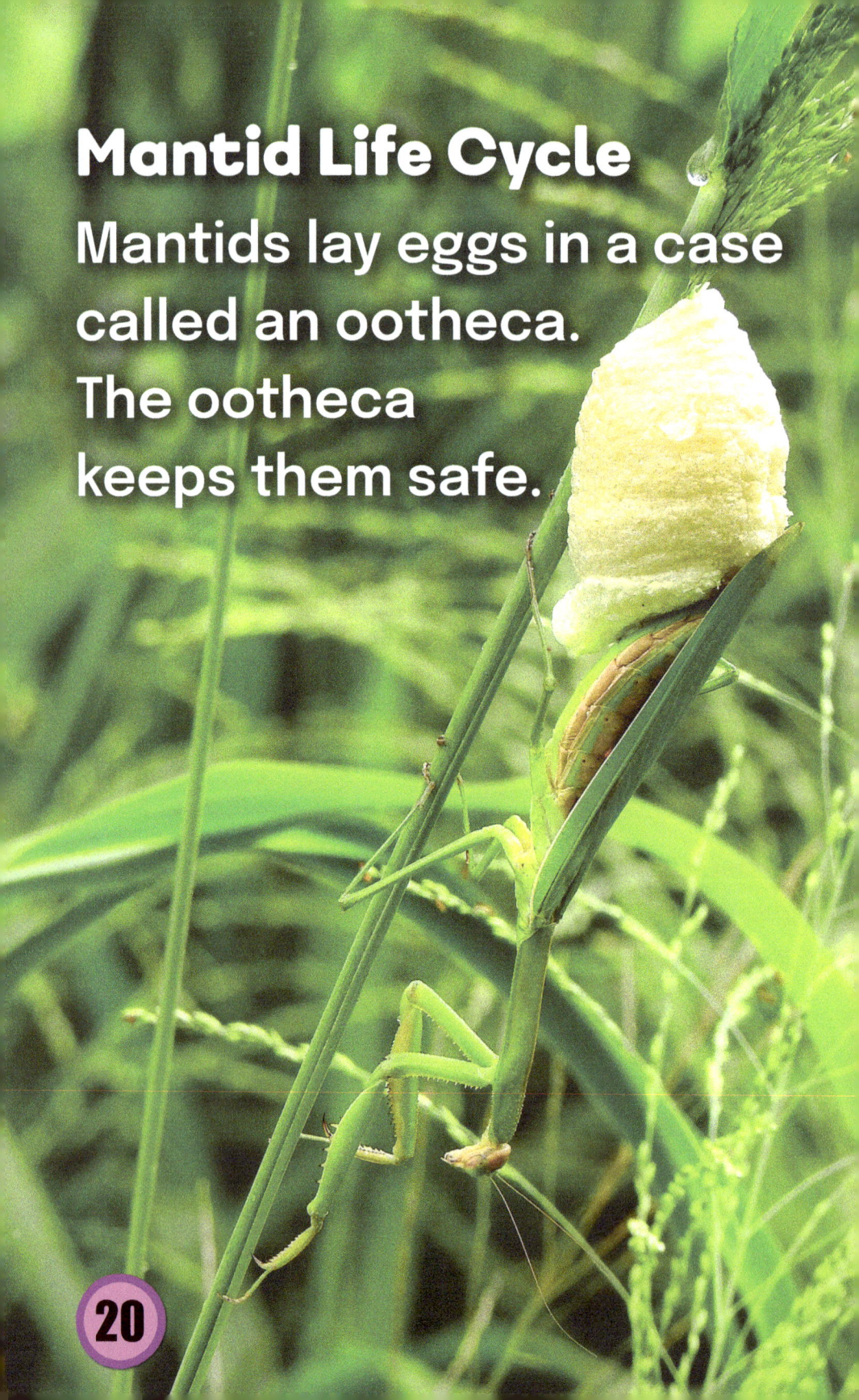

There can be up to 400 eggs in one ootheca. The eggs hatch in spring.

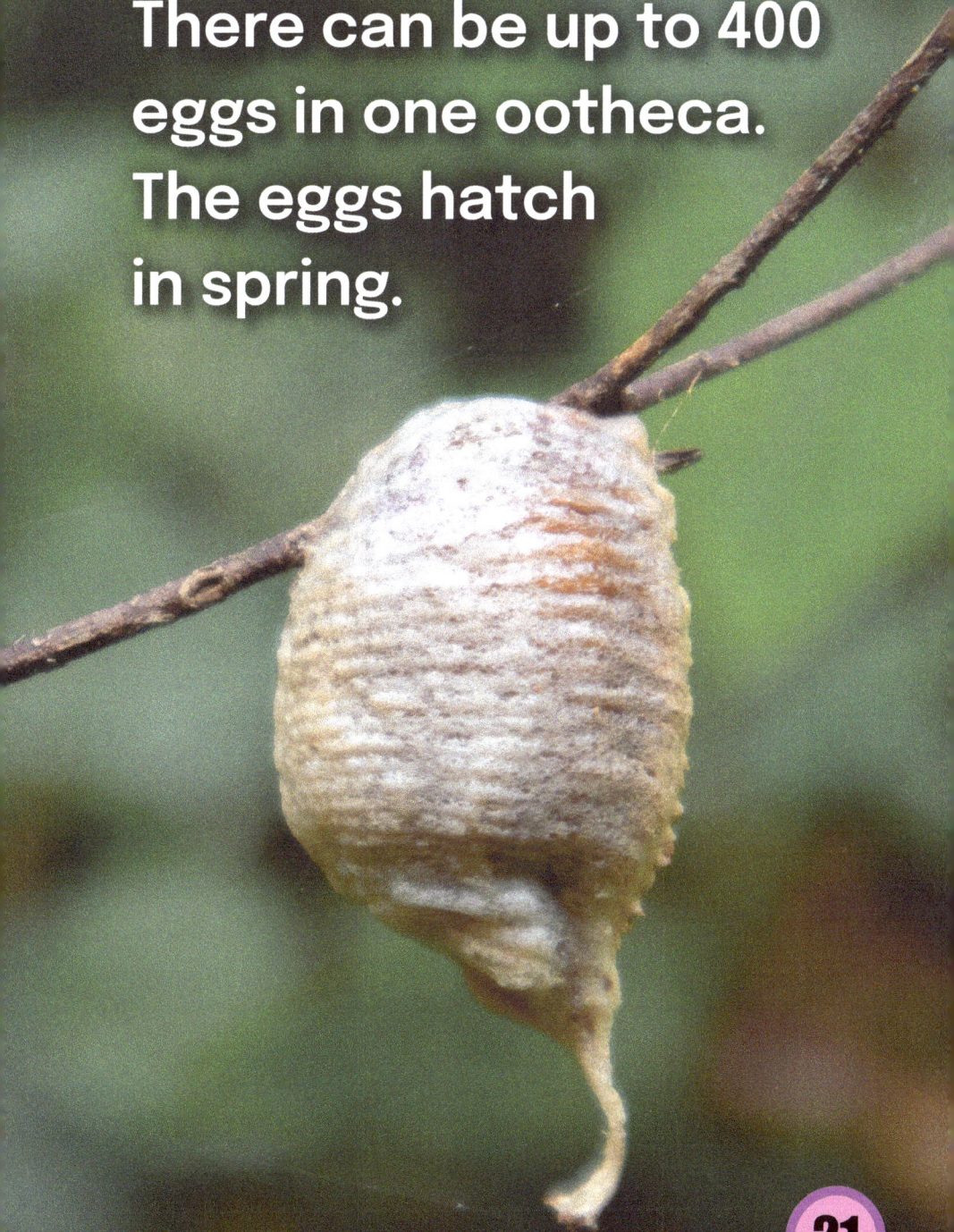

Baby mantids are called nymphs. They start to look for food as soon as they hatch.

Sometimes nymphs will eat each other. Many mantids do not live past their first winter.

Fun Facts

Mantids often eat the head of their prey first.

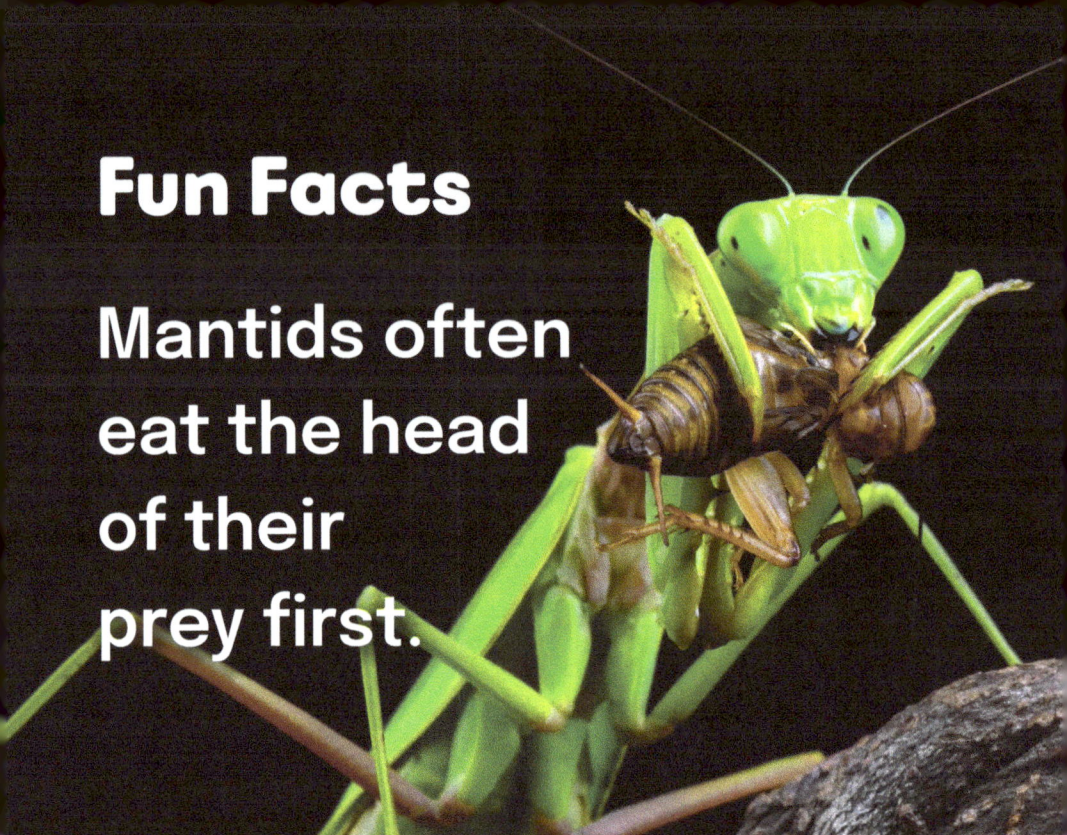

Mantids are the only insects that can turn their heads from side to side.

Nymphs can jump from point A to point B in less than half a second!

Mantids are related to cockroaches.

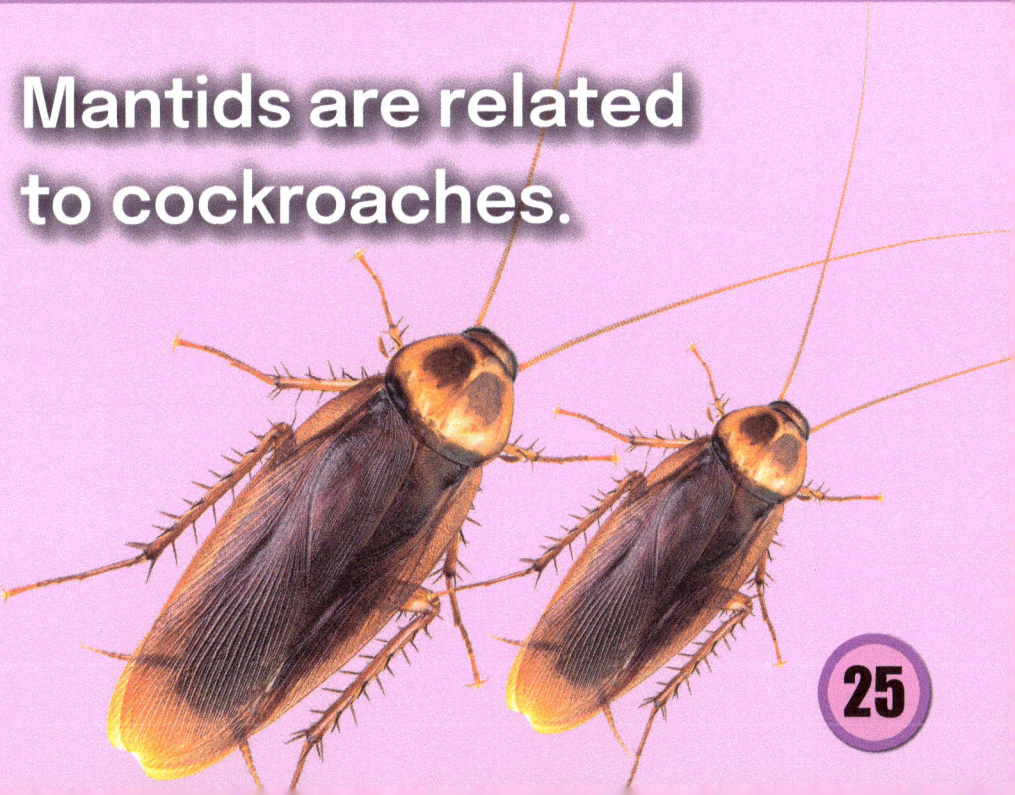

Are Mantids Helpful or Harmful?

Mantids are both helpful and harmful. They often eat bugs like beetles that harm gardens.

But mantids also eat bugs that help gardens. Bugs like bees and butterflies help plants grow and make more food for people.

Are Praying Mantids in Danger?

Most kinds of mantids are not in danger. But some kinds are.

People destroy the places where mantids live. Mantids then have nowhere to go.

28

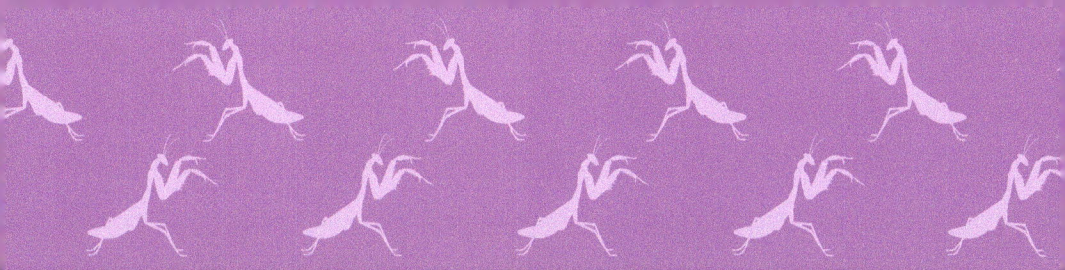

Quiz

Test your knowledge of praying mantids by answering the following questions. The questions are based on what you have read in this book. The answers are listed on the bottom of the next page.

1 Are praying mantids insects?

2 Can all mantids use their wings?

3 Do most mantids chase their food?

4 Are mantids good at hiding from other animals?

5 Are baby mantids called nymphs?

6 Are mantids related to cockroaches?

Explore other books in the
Backyard Bugs & Creepy Crawlies series!

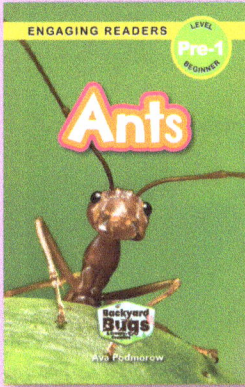

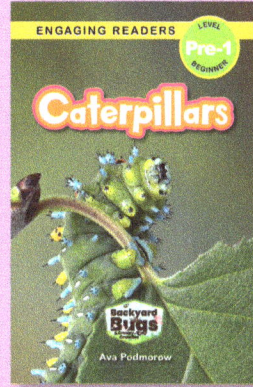

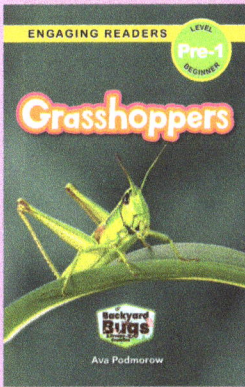

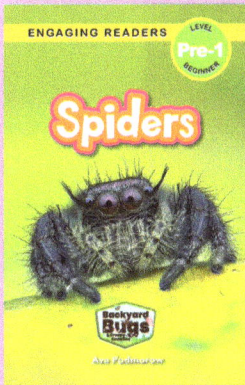

Visit www.engagebooks.com to explore more Engaging Readers.